1 Introduction and Literature Review

Does market power facilitate innovation? If so, under what circumstances should competition policy tolerate the short-term allocative inefficiency associated with market power in order to obtain higher levels of innovation? These two questions have been a central issue in Industrial Organization for 50 years. While simple answers have proved elusive, numerous papers have made significant progress toward addressing these questions. Our paper seeks to add to this stock of knowledge by considering how product market competition affects innovation when managerial compensation is a linear function of firm profits.

Changes in the intensity of product market competition affect both the return from innovation and the cost of inducing managers to innovate. An extensive literature examines the effect of product market competition on the return from innovation and finds that greater product market innovation can lead to either increased innovation or decreased innovation depending on the assumptions made about factors such as the nature of competition before and after the innovation, whether the innovation can be readily copied, and whether rivals can also innovate. (see e.g., Arrow (1962); Tirole (1988); Schumpeter (1947); Qiu (1997); Vives (2008)). Another set of paper examines the effect of product market competition on the cost of inducing managerial effort and finds that increased competition, measured as the number of entrepreneurial firms (i.e., without agency problems), either reduces agency problems or increases agency problems depending on the agent's utility function (e.g., Oliver Hart (1983) and Scharfstein (1988)). Finally, several recent papers account for both the returns-to-investment effect and agency-cost effect in analyzing the effect of additional product market competition on incentives to innovate (see e.g., Schmidt (1997), Raith (2003), and Piccolo, D'Amato, and Martina (2008)).

Similar to this last set of papers (especially Piccolo et al.), we examine the overall effect that product market competition has on innovation in the presence of managerial contracts. However, our model differs from these papers in the type of contract that we assume firms can use to induce innovation. These other models focus on the case where a firm can tailor a contract to induce managers to attain a profit or cost target associated with some particular level of innovation. In contrast, we assume that firms are restricted to using linear profit-sharing contracts with their managers. While linear contracts are clearly a special case, representing one extreme of how contracts can be written, economic theory[1] and empirical studies[2] suggest that this special case oftentimes does not differ far from reality.

With linear profit-sharing contracts, the cost of a non-drastic innovation declines as product market competition increases because the increment gained from innovation becomes a larger fraction of the total profit.[3] To see this, suppose a firm can only get a manager to undertake a project by offering this manager a share of profits. Then, the manager's share of overall profits must be sufficiently high that the manager's share of the incremental profits generated by the innovation exceeds the manager's cost of innovating. Now consider the case where the cost of a minor innovation equals half of the incremental profits from innovation. A monopoly firm is unlikely to undertake such an innovation because it does not want to give the manager half of its pre-existing

[1]Holmstrom and Milgrom (1987) identify some circumstances where optimal contracts are a linear function of profits. Prendergast (1999) and Milgrom (1991) show that contracts that link compensation to a specific goal (in this case some level of innovation) can divert an agent's effort from other important goals (in this case, other tasks necessary for profit maximization). Finally, Hall and Murphy (2003) note that shareholders may be reluctant to offer highly non-linear contracts because such contracts offer managers no incentive to perform in some possible states of the world.

[2]Empirical studies suggest that managerial compensation has a large linear component. Managers tend to own a large share of the stock of the firms they manage: Holderness et al. (1999) found that the mean percentage of common stock held by a firm's officers and directors was 21 percent in 1995. Returns on this stock comprise a large component of managers' incentive compensation: Hall and Liebman (1998) pp. 674-5 found that returns on stock and stock options account for nearly all of the relationship between managerial compensation and firm performance and that the return on stock accounts for over half of such incentive compensation. While the returns on stock options could be highly non-linear in theory, Hall and Murphy (2003) (pp. 50,59) found that "most employee stock options expire in ten years and are granted with an exercise price equal to the market price on the date of the grant." The value of such an option would be captured by an upward sloping curve positioned between the value of the share price and the value of the call option if exercised immediately. (See Brealey and Myers (1988) p. 480). Thus, the relationship between the value of these options and the firm's overall profit is closer to linear than it may initially seem. Hall and Murphy (2003) also note that stock options indexed to a competitor's stock price are "nonexistent" as an empirical phenomenon.

[3]Piccolo et al. also find that the cost of inducing effort using profit-based compensation falls as competition increases. However, a different mechanism leads to this result in their paper. Specifically, in their model, an increase in competition (as measured by product substitutability) makes firms more similar thereby making it easier for owners to determine if their manager exerted effort.

monopoly profits to get half the benefit from a minor innovation. In contrast, a firm in a more competitive market might innovate because its pre-existing profits are much smaller relative to the incremental profit from innovation.

In this paper, we argue that this decline in the cost of attaining innovation as competition increases means that competition will often lead to more innovation even in models where the returns to innovation otherwise would fall as competition increases. To show this, we use a model in which two symmetric firms, both of which can innovate, compete as differentiated Bertrand competitors and face a linear-quadratic demand function. While the additional profit that a firm gains by innovating declines as competition increases in this model (e.g., see Qiu (1997) and Piccolo et al. (2008)), once we account for the cost of attaining innovation (assuming linear profit sharing contracts), the overall return on innovation increases with competition over a wide range of parameter values.

It is sometimes argued that antitrust policy should tolerate the short-term allocative inefficiency associated with monopolies in order to gain the benefits associated with higher levels of innovation. However, our results suggest that a firm with market power may be less able to exploit such opportunities for innovation because, with market power, it is more costly to incentivize managers to innovate. This suggests that antitrust policy should be less willing to tolerate monopolies to increase the incentives to innovate than would otherwise be the case. That said, there may still be instances where greater market power is needed to encourage innovation. For instance, Qiu (among others) has noted that spillover effects of innovation can rapidly decrease a firm's incentive to innovate.

2 Model

We consider a three stage model: In stage one, each of two symmetric firms simultaneously can contract with its manager to make an investment that would lower its marginal cost; in stage two, these managers simultaneously decide whether to undertake costly investments to lower marginal cost; and, in stage three, these managers simultaneously select prices so as to maximize firm profits.

Focusing initially on stage 1, we assume that firm i's profit, π_i, is divided between its risk-neutral owner (principal), who is the residual claimant, and its risk-neutral manager (agent), who is compensated by a linear profit-sharing contract of the form of the form $w_i = b_i \pi_i$ where $b_i \in \mathbb{R}_+$. We assume for simplicity that the agent's reservation wage is zero since we only wish to examine the principal's incentive to induce the agent to undertake an action.[4] We assume that managers know the model and the previous actions of themselves and their rivals. We assume that owners know the model but cannot observe the actions of managers.[5] Given these assumptions, we then assume owners simultaneously select b_i in order to maximize expected profit.

In stage 2, managers simultaneously decide whether to undertake costly investments to reduce their constant marginal costs from their initial level αc, where $\alpha > 0$ is a scaling parameter and $0 < c < 1$. Firm i's manager can either expend effort at utility cost g to reduce i's marginal cost by αx to $\alpha(c \ \square \ x)$ (where $0 < x < c$) or expend no effort and have marginal cost remain αc. We denote the choice variable for i as $x_i \in \{0, x\}$.

In stage 3, we assume that the firms compete as differentiated Bertrand competitors.

---

[4] This justifies the zero intercept of the contract since the principle will set the assured wage to zero.

[5] These assumption are made to construct an agency problem, but we could justify them by modeling costs directly by assuming that firms can observe total costs but cannot allocate these costs between fixed and variable costs. Suppose firm i has constant marginal costs c_i and fixed cost f_i, where f_i is stochastic and distributed according to some distribution. Thus, the firm cannot infer the actions of the manager from marginal costs levels, which to it are unobservable, or from total costs, which include the stochastic fixed cost term.

Specifically, we assume that each firm i with competitor j faces a linear-quadratic demand function given by:[6]

$$D_i(p_i, p_j) = \frac{1}{1-\gamma^2}\left(\alpha\left(1-\gamma\right)-p_i+\gamma p_j\right) \text{ with } 0<\gamma<1 \qquad (1)$$

Where p_i is the price set by firm i, p_j is the price set by firm j, and γ is a parameter measuring the degree of product differentiation. The degree of product differentiation decreases with γ and thus competition between the firms increases with γ.

We limit our analysis to non-drastic innovation of the following form: we assume that x is small enough that both firms always produce a positive quantity. This assumption is equivalent to the more analytically tractable assumption that $\gamma < \bar{\gamma}$, where $\bar{\gamma}$ is the highest γ such that $q^* \geq 0$ for a firm that is at a cost disadvantage from not investing when its rival did.[7]

Assumption 1 $\gamma < \bar{\gamma} \equiv \frac{1}{2}\left(\sqrt{\frac{x(2-2c+x)}{(1-c)^2}+9}-\frac{1-c+x}{1-c}\right)$

The profit function of a firm is: $\pi_i = D_i(p_i, p_j)(p_i - MC_i)$. Thus, the firm's profit is $\pi_i = D_i(p_i, p_j)(p_i - \alpha(c-x))$ if the manager innovates and $\pi_i = D_i(p_i, p_j)(p_i - \alpha c)$ if the manager does not innovate

The equilibrium concept is subgame perfect Nash equilibrium in pure strategies, which we solve using backward induction. Since investment has a discrete size as in Bester and Petrakis (1993), we investigate how the maximum cost at which a firm would innovate changes as γ changes. In other words, we examine how the range of g under which there is equilibrium investment changes with γ rather than how the optimal size

---

[6] This demand function can also be rewritten as: $D_i(p_i, p_j) = \frac{(1-\gamma)}{1-\gamma^2}\left(\alpha - p_i + \frac{\gamma}{(1-\gamma)}(p_j - p_i)\right)$.

[7] Specifically, we assume $x < Min[\bar{x}, c]$ where $\bar{x} = \gamma^{-1}\left(2-2c\gamma+c-\gamma^2+c\gamma^2\right)$. The non-drastic constraint is not binding from $\bar{x} > c$ if $\gamma < \frac{1}{2}\left(\sqrt{8+(1-c)^{-2}}-(1-c)^{-1}\right)$.

6

of the investment changes with .

In particular, we focus the analysis on the region of g's where it is the unique pure strategy equilibrium for both owners to induce both managers to invest (given a pure strategy equilibrium in stage 2). Although we do make note of some behavior outside this region, we focus on this case for simplicity, since there are not the multiple equilibria that exist in other regions, and because when the game leaves this region, it is certain that innovation has decreased since innovation was at a maximum. In addition, the region may be of interest because it represents the region where innovation lowers production cost for all of the industry and thus the region where consumers benefit most from such innovation.

3   Innovation Effort without an Agency Problem

We begin by considering the case where an owner directly manages the firm. This case serves as a benchmark for comparison of the case with profit-sharing contracts.

Looking forward in stage 2, the Bertrand-Nash equilibrium price in stage 3 given by efforts x_i and x_j is:

$$p_i\left(x_i, x_j\right) = \frac{\alpha}{4 \square^{2}}{}^{\square}2(c \square x_i) + (c \square x_j) + {}^{\square}2 \square \square {}^{2}))\tag{2}$$

The equilibrium profit given the efforts x_i and x_j is:

$$\pi_i\left(x_i, x_j\right) = \frac{\alpha^2}{\left(4 \square {}^{2}\right)^2\left(1 \square {}^{2}\right)}{}^{\square}(\square 2 +) (c \square x_i) + (c \square x_j) + {}^{\square}2 \square \square {}^{2}))^2\tag{3}$$

Denote $\Delta\pi_{asym} = \pi_i\left(x, 0\right) \square \pi_i\left(0, 0\right)$, as the profitability of firm i innovating when firm j does not innovate, and $\Delta\pi_{sym} = \pi_i\left(x, x\right) \square \pi_i\left(0, x\right)$, as the profitability of firm i innovating when firm j innovates. Then:

$$\Delta\pi_{asym}\left(\ ,\alpha,x,c\right) = \frac{\alpha x\left(2\square^2\right)}{\left(4\square^2\right)^2\left(1\square^2\right)}\ \square\ \square\ x\ 2\square^2\big) + 2\left(1\square c\right)\ 2\square\ \square^2\big)\big) \tag{4}$$

$$\Delta\pi_{sym}\left(\ ,\alpha,x,c\right) = \Delta\pi_{asym}\left(\ ,\alpha,x,c\right)\square\frac{2\alpha^2 x^2\left(2\square^2\right)}{\left(4\square^2\right)^2\left(1\square^2\right)} \tag{5}$$

Note from equations 4 and 5 that $\Delta\pi_{asym} > \Delta\pi_{sym}$ since the extra term in $\Delta\pi_{sym}$ is negative for > 0. Since $\Delta\pi_{asym}$ is the incentive to innovate when a firm's rival does not innovate and $\Delta\pi_{sym}$ is the incentive to innovate when a firm's rival innovates, $\Delta\pi_{asym} > \Delta\pi_{sym}$ means that innovation can be thought of as strategic substitutes.

The types of equilibria are determined by several parameter regions. If and only if $\Delta\pi_{sym} > g$, investing is the dominant strategy for both firms. If $\Delta\pi_{asym} > g$ but $\Delta\pi_{sym} < g$, then there are two pure-strategy asymmetric Nash equilibria. In these equilibria, investment reduces the cost of only the investing firm's output.[8] Finally if and only if $\Delta\pi_{asym} < g$, then declining to invest is a dominant strategy for both firms.

The effect of increasing the intensity of competition (increasing) is that the equilibrium weakly moves in the direction of less innovation investment when considering the extent of the symmetric both-invest region, but the equilibrium may move in either direction when considering the extent of the asymmetric one-invest region.

Proposition 1 $\Delta\pi_{sym} > 0$, *and as   increases, $\Delta\pi_{sym}$ decreases; while, $\Delta\pi_{asym} > 0$, and as   increases, $\Delta\pi_{asym}$ decreases then increases.   Furthermore, $\Delta\pi_{sym}\left(^-\right) < \Delta\pi_{sym}\left(0\right) = \Delta\pi_{asym}\left(0\right) < \Delta\pi_{asym}\left(^-\right)$*

Proof. See Appendix. ∎

---

[8]There is also one mixed strategy equilibrium (firm i and j invest with some probability). In the mixed strategy equilibrium, investment reduces the cost of all output in the market if both firms invest, reduces the cost of only the output of the investing firm if one firm invests, and does not reduce cost if neither firm invests.

Let us first focus only on the case where it is the unique pure strategy equilibrium for both owners to invest. In this case, proposition 1 shows that an owner's additional profit from having a lower marginal cost declines as   (competition) increases and thus the amount that an owner would invest to achieve this lower marginal cost also declines as   increases. (This is also shown in figure 1). This result, variants of which are noted by Qui (1997) and Piccolo et al. (2008), supports the Schumpeterian view that market power leads to greater innovation. This result, however, only describes how the benefit from innovating (the additional profit from having a lower marginal cost) changes as competition increases. To understand how a firm's overall profit from innovating changes as competition increases, we must also consider how the cost of attaining such innovation changes as competition increases. The next section does this using this result as a benchmark. As noted earlier, we focus on the case where both firms innovate because it represents the region where innovation lowers production cost for all of the industry and thus the region where consumers benefit most from such innovation.

For example, assuming $\alpha = 1$, $c = 1/4$, and $x = 1/20$, then the return to investing when the rival invests is shown by the figure 1.

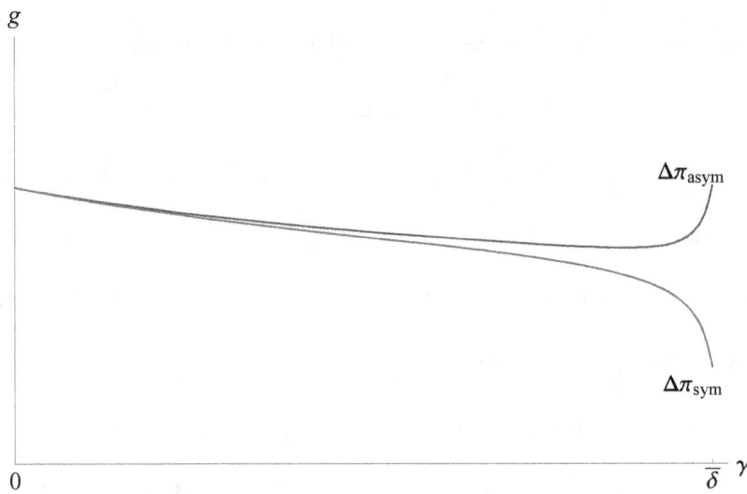

Figure 1: Baseline Example: $\Delta\pi_{asym}$ and $\Delta\pi_{sym}$ for

$$(\alpha, c, x) = \left(1, \tfrac{1}{4}, \tfrac{1}{20}\right)$$

As an aside, let us now briefly consider the parameter region where it is a pure strategy equilibrium for only one owner to invest. Proposition 1 shows that an owner's additional profit from having a lower marginal cost first decreases and then increases as competition ( ) increases. Combining this result with the result for the case where both owners invest, and recalling that $\Delta\pi_{asym} > \Delta\pi_{sym}$, shows that the form of the equilibrium can change in a number of ways as increases. Specifically, depending on the level of g (the cost of innovating), the relationship between competition and investment may result in the following: (1) no innovation for any level of competition $(g > \Delta\pi_{asym}(^-))$, (2) no innovation followed by innovation by only one firm $(\Delta\pi_{asym}(0) < g < \Delta\pi_{asym}(^-))$, (3) innovation by both firms, followed by innovation by one firm, followed by no innovation, followed by innovation by only one firm $(\min \Delta\pi_{asym} < g < \Delta\pi_{asym}(0))$, (4) innovation by both firms followed by innovation by only one firm $(\Delta\pi_{sym}(^-) < g < \min \Delta\pi_{asym})$, (5) innovation by both firms for all levels of competition $(g < \Delta\pi_{sym}(^-))$. Note that if innovation is costless, $g = 0$, then it is the dominant strategy for both firms to invest.

These results arise in large part because of the lumpiness of innovation investment. This lumpiness gives rise to asymmetric outcomes in a symmetric situation, and this asymmetry in turn leads to the increase in investment after the initial decrease. If investment was not lumpy, then as the return to investment falls with increased competition (given that the opponent is also investing) both firms would reduce investment leading potentially to a symmetric equilibrium. Since investment is lumpy, as the return to investment decreases one or both of the firms will stop investment, which creates the opportunity for an asymmetric outcome where one firm invests and the other does not. Investing when the opponent does not has a different relationship to the intensity of competition than investing when the opponent also invests because investing entails getting away from the opponent instead of matching the opponent. As the level of competition increases, the benefit of distancing from the opponent eventually increases because the baseline profit of not investing suffers greatly from the increase in competition. While we believe this last set of results are interesting, we do not use them in the remainder of the paper.

4 Principal-Agent Model: Managerial Contracts

In this section, we consider the case where the owner and the manager are separate and thus where the owner must contract with the owner to obtain innovation. Recall that the owner of firm i is constrained to use contracts of the form: $w_i = b_i \Delta \pi_i$. Thus, for innovating to be the dominant strategy for manager i, the following incentive compatibility conditions must hold.

$$b_i \Delta \pi_{asym} > g \qquad (6)$$

$$b_i \Delta\pi_{sym} > g \qquad (7)$$

Since $\Delta\pi_{asym} > \Delta\pi_{sym}$, equation 7 is the binding condition in terms of defining the region of such that innovating is a dominant strategy for managers of both firms. Define $*(g, \alpha, c, x)$ as the implicit function defined by: $\Delta\pi_{sym}(\ , \alpha, c, x) = g$. Define $**(b, g, \alpha, c, x)$ such that for all that $0 < \ < **(b, g)$, the equilibrium of the stage 2 has both managers investing as a dominant strategy. Since the manager receives only a share of the additional profit from innovating, an immediate result is that for any b, fewer situations induce both firms to invest than in the model without an agency problem:

Proposition 2 *For any $b \in (0, 1)$, $**(b, g) < *(g)$.*

Proof. From proposition 1, $\Delta\pi_{sym} > 0$, $\frac{\partial \Delta\pi_{sym}}{\partial} < 0$, and $0 < b < 1$. $\frac{\partial \Delta\pi_{sym}}{\partial} < 0$ implies that this implicit function is well-defined. If is such that $b\Delta\pi_{sym} = g$, it must be that $\Delta\pi_{sym} > g$. ∎

A second result is that an owner must pay a manager a larger share of firm profit in order to obtain innovation as competition increases. However, because the firm's overall profit decreases as competition increases, the total amount paid to managers decreases as competition increases. Denote b_{sym} as the minimum b that will induce the agent to innovate given g and the other firm investing, i.e., $b_{sym} = \frac{g}{\Delta\pi_{sym}}$.[9]

Proposition 3 *For the case where both rivals invest, when $g < \Delta\pi_{sym}$, the fraction of profits needed to induce the manager to invest increases as competition increases, $\frac{\partial b_{sym}}{\partial} > 0$, while both the payment to the manager and the return to the owner from innovating decrease, $\frac{\partial b_{sym}\pi_i(x,x)}{\partial} < 0$ and $\frac{\partial(1\square b_{sym})\pi_i(x,x)}{\partial} < 0$.*

---

[9] $b_{sym} = \dfrac{g(\ ^2 \square 4)^2(1\square\ ^2)}{x(2\square\ ^2)(2(\alpha\square c + x)(2\square\ ^2\square\ ) \square x(2\square\ ^2))}$

12

Proof. See Appendix. ∎

Denote b_{asym} as the minimum b that will induce the agent to innovate given g and the other firm not investing, i.e., $b_{asym} = \frac{g}{\Delta\pi_{asym}}$.[10] Since $\Delta\pi_{asym} > \Delta\pi_{sym}$, it is the case that $b_{sym} > b_{asym}$.

Since the principal will not pay an excess sum to induce an action, the only pure strategy equilibria of stage 1 are (b_{sym}, b_{sym}), $(b_{asym}, 0)$, $(0, b_{asym})$, and $(0, 0)$ (See Table 2.) In stage 2, the choices of b from the stage 1 determine the equilibrium investments. If the principals choose (b_{sym}, b_{sym}) then investing is a dominant strategy for both agents, and thus (x, x) is the unique stage 2 Nash Equilibrium. If the principals choose (b_{sym}, b_{asym}) then investing remains the dominant strategy for the agent of firm 1. However, since the agent for firm 2 will only invest when the agent for firm 1 declines to invest, the unique stage 2 Nash Equilibrium is now $(x, 0)$. Therefore, an equilibrium is not formed by (b_{sym}, b_{asym}) because principal 2 would unilaterally deviate to $(b_{sym}, 0)$ since $\pi_2(0, x) > (1 \square b_{asym})\pi_2(0, x)$, similarly for (b_{asym}, b_{sym}). If the principals choose $(b_{sym}, 0)$ then investing is a dominant strategy for the agent of firm 1 while not investing is a dominant strategy for the agent of firm 2. Thus, the unique stage 2 Nash Equilibrium is $(x, 0)$. However, an equilibrium is not formed by $(b_{sym}, 0)$ because principal 1 would unilaterally deviate to $(b_{asym}, 0)$ since $(1 \square b_{asym})\pi_1(0, x) > (1 \square b_{sym})\pi_1(0, x)$, similarly for $(0, b_{sym})$. If the principals choose (b_{asym}, b_{asym}) then, there are two pure strategy Nash equilibria: $(x, 0)$ and $(0, x)$. Therefore, an equilibrium is not formed by (b_{asym}, b_{asym}) (with a pure strategy equilibrium in stage 2) because the principal whose agent does not invest in stage 2 would unilaterally deviate from b_{asym} to 0 since $\pi_i(0, x) > (1 \square b_{asym})\pi_i(0, x)$. If the principals choose $(0, 0)$ then for both agents not investing is a dominant strategy, thus the unique Nash equilibrium is $(0, 0)$. Neither b_{sym} nor b_{asym} is ever a dominant strategy in stage 1 because in response to 0

---

[10] $b_{asym} = \frac{g(4\square^2)^2(1\square^2)}{x(2\square^2)((+2)(2(\alpha\square c+x)(1\square)+x)\square 2x)}$

13

and b_{sym} (respectively) another strategy may give a higher payoff.

Stage 1 has (b_{sym}, b_{sym}) as an equilibrium if incentive condition 8 holds.

$$(1 \square b_{sym}) \pi_i (x, x) > \pi_i (0, x) \tag{8}$$

Stage 1 has $(b_{asym}, 0)$ or $(0, b_{asym})$ as an equilibrium, if incentive conditions 9 and 10 hold.

$$(1 \square b_{asym}) \pi_i (x, 0) > \pi_i (0, 0) \tag{9}$$

$$\pi_j (0, x) > (1 \square b_{sym}) \pi_j (x, 0) \tag{10}$$

Stage 1 has $(0, 0)$ as an equilibrium if the negation of 9 holds.

There is a unique (b_{sym}, b_{sym}) equilibrium if condition 8 holds as well as condition 9 and the negation of 10.[11]

We find that for any set of parameter values $(\alpha, c, x, \ )$, there is a level of investment cost, g_{sym}, such that for $g < g_{sym}$, the unique pure strategy equilibrium is for both owners to induce their managers to invest. Furthermore, we find that g_{sym}, which defines a parametric threshold beyond which investment decreases, has a non-monotonic relationship to the intensity of competition ( ). Generally as competition increases, g_{sym} declines at first when competition is low, then increases as competition intensifies, and finally declines as competition further intensifies. (See figures 2, 3, and 4). We find that the region where increased competition leads to greater innovation increases in extent as c and x fall but does not depend on α. Thus, the effect in which greater

---

[11]There is a unique $(b_{asym}, 0)$ or $(0, b_{asym})$ equilibrium if conditions 9 and 10 hold as well as the negation of condition 8. There is a unique $(0, 0)$ equilibrium if the negation of condition 9 holds as well as the negation of condition 8. With the negation of conditions 9 and 8, stage 1 has $b_i = 0$ as a dominant strategy, and therefore $(0, 0)$ as the unique equilibrium, if condition 10 holds.

competition leads to greater innovation is most extensive where cost is relatively low and where innovation leads to relatively small cost reductions.

Proposition 4 *There is $g_{sym}(\alpha, c, x, \theta)$ such that if $g < g_{sym}$ then the unique (pure strategy) equilibrium is for both principals to induce the agents to invest by setting $b^* = b_{sym}$ and if $g > g_{sym}$ then both principals inducing investment is not an equilibrium. There is an $\bar{x}$ and a $\bar{c}(x)$ such that if $x < \bar{x}$ and $c < \bar{c}(x)$, then there are $\theta_L(c, x)$ and $\theta_U(c, x)$ such that $\frac{\partial g_{sym}}{\partial \theta} > 0$ if $\theta_L < \theta < \theta_U$; otherwise $\frac{\partial g_{sym}}{\partial \theta} \leq 0$.[12] Finally, $\frac{\partial \theta_L}{\partial \alpha} = 0$, $\frac{\partial \theta_L}{\partial c} > 0$, $\frac{\partial \theta_L}{\partial x} > 0$, $\frac{\partial \theta_U}{\partial \alpha} = 0$, $\frac{\partial \theta_U}{\partial c} < 0$, and $\frac{\partial \theta_U}{\partial x} < 0$.*

Proof. See Appendix. ∎

---

[12]For instance at $\theta = \frac{1}{2}$, then $\frac{\partial g_{sym}}{\partial \theta} > 0$ if $x < \frac{190}{511}$ and $c < 1 - \frac{321}{190}x$.

The results from proposition 4 can also be visualized through two examples in which g_{sym} declines slightly over a narrow range when competition is low, increases significantly over a broad range as competition intensifies, and finally declines sharply as competition further intensifies. In example 1, $\alpha = 1, c = \frac{1}{3}, x = \frac{1}{6}$, thus an innovation would reduce marginal cost by 50 percent. In this example, the highest level of cost for which a firm with an agent would invest when its rival also invests (g_{sym}) initially falls almost imperceptibly, then rises over almost the entire range of the substitution parameter , then falls sharply as competition becomes very intense. In example 2, $\alpha = 1, c = \frac{1}{2}, x = \frac{1}{5}$, thus, an innovation would reduce marginal cost by 40 percent. In this example, g_{sym} declines modestly when the substitution parameter is low, increases substantially when the substitution parameter has moderate values, and then falls sharply for very high levels of substitution. As we noted earlier, the effect in which greater competition leads to greater innovation is strongest when cost is low relative to demand and where innovation leads to relatively small cost reductions. These two examples in particular show that the the competition effect is substantial and extensive for reasonable parameter values.

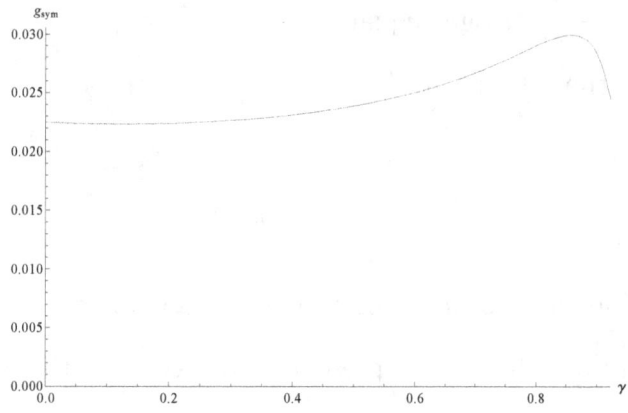

Figure 3: Example 1: $(\alpha, c, x) = \left(1, \frac{1}{3}, \frac{1}{6}\right)$

17

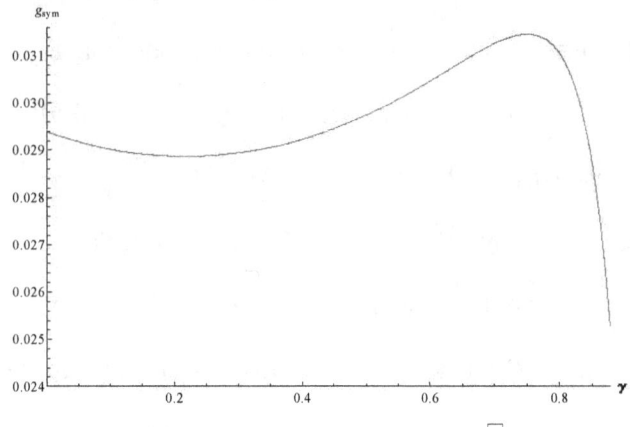

Figure 4: Example 2: $(\alpha, c, x) = \left(1, \frac{1}{2}, \frac{1}{5}\right)$

In our model, the relationship between product market competition and innovation changes dramatically when we add the assumption that firms can only use profit-sharing contracts to motivate managers to innovate: Absent agency problems, the level of innovation declines monotonically with greater product market competition; when firms must use profit-sharing contracts to solve agency problems, the level of innovation initially declines slightly, then rises over a broad region, and then falls sharply.

The intuition for this result can be seen by combining the equality formed by condition 8 and $b_{sym} = \frac{g}{\Delta \pi_{sym}}$ to get equation 11, where $\pi_R = \frac{\Delta \pi_{sym}}{\pi(x,x)}$ (the ratio of the incremental profit to the total profit).

$$g_{sym} = \Delta \pi_{sym} * \pi_R \tag{11}$$

Equation 11 divides g_{sym} into a factor that represents the benefit of inducing innovation, $\Delta \pi_{sym}$, and a factor that represents the inverse of the cost to the owner of inducing innovation, π_R. Intuitively, the owner must offer the agent a sufficiently high share of total profits that the agent's share of incremental profits exceeds the cost of innovation. Therefore, the cost of inducing innovation depends on the ratio of the

18

incremental profit to the total profit because the owner will pay a fraction of the total but the size of the fraction depends on the size of the increment relative to g.[13]

The change of the boundary of the investment region, $\frac{\partial g_{sym}}{\partial}$, can then be written as in equation 12 (since $\frac{\partial \Delta \pi_{sym}}{\partial} < 0$ and $\frac{\partial \pi_R}{\partial} > 0$ from Proposition 3).[14]

$$\frac{\partial g_{sym}}{\partial} = \square \left| \frac{\partial \Delta \pi_{sym}}{\partial} \right| \pi_R + \left| \frac{\partial \pi_R}{\partial} \right| \Delta \pi_{sym} \tag{12}$$

The maximum cost where both firms innovate decreases with competition if and only if $\left| \frac{\partial \Delta \pi_{sym}}{\partial} \right| \pi_R$ is greater than $\left| \frac{\partial \pi_R}{\partial} \right| \Delta \pi_{sym}$. In other words, if the effect of the decrease in the incremental profit is greater than the effect of the decrease in the cost of investing multiplier (relative to the levels) then investment decreases with competition. This can be understood as the decrease in the return to innovation dominating the decrease in the cost of inducing innovation. The maximum cost where both invest increases with competition if $\left| \frac{\partial \pi_R}{\partial} \right| \Delta \pi_{sym} > \left| \frac{\partial \Delta \pi_{sym}}{\partial} \right| \pi_R$. This can be understood as the decrease in the cost of inducing innovation dominating the decrease in the return to innovation. Therefore, the non-monotonic relationship between product market competition and innovation results from one effect being dominant over the other for some ranges of competitive intensity but not all.

---

[13]Formally, the cost can be divided into two parts, a fraction of the incremental profit and a fraction of the baseline profit. The fraction of the incremental profit must equal g to induce innovation, which determines b_{sym}. This same fraction of the baseline profit also becomes part of the cost. Therefore for a given level of incremental profit, if the baseline profit decreases then the cost decreases because the necessary fraction stayed the same but the total payment decreased. Alternatively, for a given level of total profit, as more of the profit is shifted into the increment from the baseline, the necessary fraction of the total decreases since g stayed the same but $\Delta \pi_{sym}$ increased and therefore the cost decreases (because the total profit stayed the same).

[14]In proposition 3, we find $\frac{\partial b_{sym} \pi_i(x,x)}{\partial} < 0$, which is equivalent to $g \frac{\partial (1/\pi_R)}{\partial} < 0$.

5   Generalization for Profit Functions

This section considers the generality of our results by deriving conditions for general (stage 2) profit functions under which the incentive effects driving our results hold. First, the cost of innovation, $b_{sym}\pi(x,x)$, can be divided into two parts: (1) the satisfaction of the incentive compatibility constraint: $b_{sym}\Delta\pi_{sym}$ and (2) a rent to the manager: $b_{sym}(\pi(x,x) \square \Delta\pi_{sym}) = b_{sym}\pi(0,x)$.[15] The incentive compatibility constraint payment is constant with respect to since $b_{sym}(\ )\Delta\pi_{sym}(\ ) = g$. Only the rent to the manager, $b_{sym}(\ )\pi(0,x)(\ )$, changes with intensity of competition. From the incentive compatibility constraint, $b_{sym} = \frac{g}{\Delta\pi_{sym}}$, so the manager's rent is equal to $\frac{g}{\Delta\pi_{sym}(\ )}\pi(0,x)(\ )$.

Proposition 4 follows from the cost of inducing innovation decreasing with competition due to profit sharing contracts, which occurs if and only if Condition 13 holds.[16]

$$\frac{\partial\pi(x,x)/\partial}{\pi(x,x)} > \frac{\partial\pi(0,x)/\partial}{\pi(0,x)} \tag{13}$$

Condition 13 requires that an increase in the intensity of competition has a more negative proportional effect on the profit of not matching the innovation of the rival than the profit of matching it so that the incremental profit decreases less than the baseline profit–increasing the ratio of the incremental profit to the total profit. With constant marginal costs, Condition 13 can be refined. Using the envelope theorem, the cost of innovation decreases with the intensity of competition if and only if Condition 14 holds (abusing some notation).[17]

---

[15] Inducing innovation when the opponent innovates is worthwhile only if $(1\square b_{sym})\pi(x,x) > \pi(0,x)$, which can be rewritten as $\Delta\pi_{sym} > b_{sym}\pi(x,x)$–the return being greater than the cost.

[16] Since $\partial\frac{g}{\Delta\pi_{sym}(\ )}\pi(0,x)(\ )/\partial = g\frac{(\pi(x,x)\square\pi(0,x))(\partial\pi(0,x)/\partial\ )\square\pi(0,x)(\partial\pi(x,x)/\partial\ \square\partial\pi(0,x)/\partial\ )}{(\pi(x,x)\square\pi(0,x))^2}$

which simplifies to $g\frac{\pi(x,x)(\partial\pi(0,x)/\partial\ )\square\pi(0,x)(\partial\pi(x,x)/\partial\ )}{(\pi(x,x)\square\pi(0,x))^2}$, the overall effect on cost is negative if and only if $\pi(x,x)(\partial\pi(0,x)/\partial\ ) < \pi(0,x)(\partial\pi(x,x)/\partial\ )$.

[17] Since from the hypothesis x_i and x_j are fixed:

$\partial\pi_i/\partial = \left(\left(\frac{\partial p_i^*}{\partial}\right)\left(D_i + (p_i^*\square c + x_i^*)\frac{\partial D_i}{\partial p_i^*}\right) + (p_i^*\square c + x_i^*)\left(\frac{\partial D_i}{\partial p_j^*}\frac{\partial p_j^*}{\partial} + \frac{\partial D_i}{\partial}\right)\right)$.   From the FOC's:

$$\left(\frac{\partial D_i(x,x)}{\partial p_j^*} \frac{\partial p_j^*(x,x)}{\partial} + \frac{\partial D_i(x,x)}{\partial} \right) / D_i(x,x)$$
$$> \left(\frac{\partial D_i(0,x)}{\partial p_j^*} \frac{\partial p_j^*(x,0)}{\partial} + \frac{\partial D_i(0,x)}{\partial} \right) / D_i(0,x) \tag{14}$$

If the cost of innovation is decreasing, then overall innovation increases with competition if either the return to innovation increases with competition or if the cost of innovation falls more quickly than the return. In a model such as Singh-Vives (1984), where the return to innovation increases with competition, the cost reducing effect of profit sharing contracts simply amplifies the increasing return to innovation. In a Schumpeterian model where the return to innovation falls with competition (such as the one we consider), the rates of change of the return and the cost must be compared.

The cost decreases more quickly than the return to innovation as   increases if and only if 15 holds at a given g.

$$g \frac{\pi(x,x)\left(\partial\pi(0,x)/\partial\right) \square \pi(0,x)\left(\partial\pi(x,x)/\partial\right)}{\left(\pi(x,x) \square \pi(0,x)\right)^2} < \left(\frac{\partial\pi(x,x)}{\partial} \square \frac{\partial\pi(0,x)}{\partial} \right) \tag{15}$$

The extent of the both invest region expands with   if there is an increase in the highest g such that $\Delta\pi_{sym} \geq b_{sym}\pi(x,x)$. The highest such g is g_{sym} defined earlier, and then condition 15 yields condition 16. More stringent than Condition 13, Condition 16 requires that the proportional effect on profit when both invest be less negative than a proportional effect on the laggard, where the laggard effect is less negative than in 13 since it is proportional to the average of the two profits.[18] Intuitively, this condition requires that the cost of inducing innovation not only decreases as in Condition 13 but

---

$\left(D_i + (p_i^* \square c + x_i^*)\frac{\partial D_i}{\partial p_i^*} \right) = 0$, then $\partial\pi_i(x_i,x_j)/\partial = (p_i^* \square c + x_i^*)\left(\frac{\partial D_i}{\partial p_j^*}\frac{\partial p_j^*}{\partial} + \frac{\partial D_i}{\partial} \right)$. Finally, the price-cost margins cancel.

[18]Condition 16 is can be derived alternatively by taking the derivative of g_{sym} directly, yielding $\frac{\partial g_{sym}}{\partial} = \frac{(\pi(x,x)\square\pi(0,x))((\pi(x,x)+\pi(0,x))\partial\pi(x,x)/\partial \ \square \ 2\pi(x,x)\partial\pi(0,x)/\partial)}{\pi(x,x)^2} > 0.$

21

with a high enough rate.[19]

$$\frac{\partial \pi\left(x, x\right) / \partial}{\pi\left(x, x\right)} > \frac{\partial \pi\left(0, x\right) / \partial}{\left(\pi\left(x, x\right) + \pi\left(0, x\right)\right) / 2} \tag{16}$$

6 Conclusion

This paper analyzes the effect of greater product market competition on innovation using a model that makes two key assumptions. First, the model assumes that two symmetric firms, both of which can innovate, compete as differentiated Bertrand competitors and face a linear quadratic demand function. With this assumption, a firm's benefit from making a non-drastic innovation declines as product market competition increases. Second, the model assumes that a firm can only incentivize managers to innovate by offering them a fixed share of profits. With this assumption, a firm's cost of investing in a non-drastic innovation declines as product market competition increases. The overall effect of increasing product market competition in this model depends on whether the reduction-in-benefit effect or the reduction-in-cost-of-innovating effect dominates. In our paper, we find that the reduction-in-benefit effect dominates where product market competition is either very low or very high, however, the reduction-in-cost effect dominates for intermediate levels of product market competition. Based on these results and our general analysis, the argument that firms with market power are more innovative is weaker once one accounts for one plausible cost of innovating.

Of course, our finding that firms with substantial market power have a high cost of innovating is premised on the assumption that firms can only incentivize managers by offering them linear profit sharing contracts. Thus, at this point, it is useful to revisit this assumption. As noted earlier, economic theory suggests that a linear profit-sharing

---

[19]A version of Condition 14 is available but is much more cumbersome since the price-cost margins do not cancel.

contract may perform well in some circumstances, and empirical work suggests that the incentive contracts between firms and top management often have a significant linear profit-sharing component. On the other hand, if innovation is very important, a monopoly firm would have an incentive to use some other type of contract because it does not want to offer managers a significant share of pre-existing profits to gain a comparatively small incremental profit. However, these other types of incentive contracts are likely to be costly because contracts that target one particular goal can harm a firm by diverting attention from other important goals. Hence, irrespective of the incentive contract a monopoly firm uses, such a firm may find it costlier to induce innovation than would a competitive firm.

Put differently, several treatments of agency problems within firms note that agency problems are eliminated if the manager can own the firm. Compared to a monopoly firm, it is much less expensive for a competitive firm to get a manager part of the way toward this goal because the competitive firm's pre-existing profits are smaller relative to the incremental profits from innovating.

Finally, our results illustrate a more general relationship between agency problems and competition and may offer an explanation regarding the relationship of firm size and innovation productivity. If an agency problem increases the costliness of inducing innovation, then an increase in the intensity of competition may increase innovation if it reduces the size of these frictions. The type of problem we consider is that contracts are constrained to be particularly coarse, but a similar mechanism may well hold for less extreme sets of contracts or other frictions that occur from the stochastic nature of profits and multi-task nature of management. In addition, it is thought that small firms are important innovators (Gans and Stern, 2003), which is perhaps because they have an advantage in the production of research since they can more properly incentivize their research employees. Our paper shows that one reason for this could be that the frictions related to the costliness of incentivizing employees are directly related to the ratio of the incremental profit from an innovation to the total profit–a friction that would be smaller for a smaller firm or an up-and-coming firm.

	Firm 1 Profit	Firm 2 profit
(I,I)	$\pi_{I,I} = \dfrac{\alpha^2(1\square)(1\square c+x)^2}{(1+)(2\square)^2}$	$\pi_{I,I} = \dfrac{\alpha^2(1\square)(1\square c+x)^2}{(1+)(2\square)^2}$
(I,D)	$\pi_{I,D} = \dfrac{\alpha^2\left(x+(2\square\ \square^2)(1\square c+x)\right)^2}{(1\square^2)(4\square^2)^2}$	$\pi_{I,D} = \dfrac{\alpha^2\left(x\ \square(2\square\ \square^2)(1\square c)\right)^2}{(1\square^2)(4\square^2)^2}$
(D,I)	$\pi_{D,I} = \dfrac{\alpha^2\left(x\ \square(2\square\ \square^2)(1\square c)\right)^2}{(1\square^2)(4\square^2)^2}$	$\pi_{D,I} = \dfrac{\alpha^2\left(x+(2\square\ \square^2)(1\square c+x)\right)^2}{(1\square^2)(4\square^2)^2}$
(D,D)	$\pi_{D,D} = \dfrac{\alpha^2(1\square)(1\square c)^2}{(1+)(2\square)^2}$	$\pi_{D,D} = \dfrac{\alpha^2(1\square)(1\square c)^2}{(1+)(2\square)^2}$

Table 1: Stage 2 Payoffs to Investment Decision

	$b_2 = 0$	$b_2 = b_{asym}$	$b_2 = b_{sym}$
$b_1 = 0$	$\pi_1(0,0),$ $\pi_2(0,0)$	$\pi_1(0,x),$ $(1\square b_{asym})\pi_2(x,0)$	$\pi_1(0,x),$ $(1\square b_{sym})\pi_2(x,0)$
$b_1 = b_{asym}$	$(1\square b_{asym})\pi_1(x,0),$ $\pi_2(0,x)$	$(1\square b_{asym})\pi_1(x,0),$ $(1\square b_{asym})\pi_2(0,x)$	$(1\square b_{asym})\pi_1(0,x),$ $(1\square b_{sym})\pi_2(x,0)$
$b_1 = b_{sym}$	$(1\square b_{sym})\pi_1(x,0),$ $\pi_2(0,x)$	$(1\square b_{sym})\pi_1(x,0),$ $(1\square b_{asym})\pi_2(0,x)$	$(1\square b_{sym})\pi_1(x,x),$ $(1\square b_{sym})\pi_2(x,x)$

Table 2: Stage 1 Payoffs, Assuming Pure Strategy (Asymmetric) Stage 3 Equilibrium in which Manager 1 Invests.

7 Appendix

Proof. Define: $d = (1\square c)$, $f = (2d+x)$, and $h = (d+x)$.

$\Delta\pi_{sym}$: The expression for $\Delta\pi_{sym} = \frac{\alpha^2 x(2\square\ ^2)}{(1\square^2)(4\square^2)}(2d\ \square 2h\ \square 2h\ ^2)$ is the product of two factors. The first factor is always positive. The second factor has one root in the range $0 < \ < 1$: $^* = \frac{\square(1\square c+x)\square\sqrt{9(1\square c)^2+10x(1\square c)+3x^2}}{2\square 2c+x}$, such that if $0 < \ < ^*$ then $\Delta\pi_{sym} > 0$ and if $^* < \ < 1$ then $\Delta\pi_{sym} < 0$. Since $^- < \ ^*$, if $\ < ^-$ then $\Delta\pi_{sym} > 0$. The expression for $\frac{\partial\Delta\pi_{sym}}{\partial}$ is the product of two factors. The first factor, $\frac{\square 2x\alpha^2}{(4\square^2)^3(1\square^2)^2}$, is always negative. The second factor is $(8h\ \square 8f\ +2h\ ^2+8f\ ^3\ \square 7h\ ^4\ \square 4f\ ^5+3h\ ^6+f\ ^7)$. This second factor has no roots in the range in the range $0 < \ < 1$ and is positive in this range. Therefore $\frac{\partial\Delta\pi_{sym}}{\partial} < 0$.

$\Delta\pi_{asym}$: Since $\Delta\pi_{asym} > \Delta\pi_{sym}$, it is also therefore always positive. The expression $\Delta\pi_{asym}$ is continuous at $\ = 0$ and $\ = ^-$. The difference, $\Delta\pi_{asym}(^-)\square\Delta\pi_{asym}(0)$, is positive being a product of two factors: $\frac{x\alpha^2\ ^-}{4(4\square^{-2})^2(1\square^{-2})} > 0$ and a first-degree polynomial in (α, c) which is always positive. The expression for $\frac{\partial\Delta\pi_{asym}}{\partial}$ is the product of two factors. The first factor, $\frac{x(2\square\ ^2)}{(\ ^2\square 4)^2(1\square\ ^2)}$, is always positive. The second factor is: $(8d\ \square 8f\ +2d\ ^2+8f\ ^3\ \square 7d\ ^4\ \square 4f\ ^5+3d\ ^6+f\ ^7)$. This polynomial has a single

25

root in $(0, \bar{\ })$, $**$, such that if $0 < \ < **$ then $\frac{\partial \Delta \pi_{asym}}{\partial \ } > 0$ and if $** < \ < \bar{\ }$ then $\frac{\partial \Delta \pi_{asym}}{\partial \ } < 0$. Also $\Delta \pi_{sym}(0) = \Delta \pi_{asym}(0) = (1/4)\alpha^2(2 - 2c + x)$. ∎

Proof. Proposition 3

1. Since $\frac{\partial b_{sym}(\ )\Delta \pi_{sym}(\ )}{\partial \ } = \frac{\partial b_{sym}(\ )}{\partial \ }\Delta \pi_{sym}(\ ) + b_{sym}(\ )\frac{\partial \Delta \pi_{sym}(\ )}{\partial \ } = \frac{\partial g}{\partial \ } = 0$ and $\frac{\partial \Delta \pi_{sym}(\ )}{\partial \ } < 0$, therefore it must be the case that $\frac{\partial b_{sym}(\ )}{\partial \ } > 0$.

2. $\frac{\partial b_{sym}(\ )\pi_i(x,x)(\ )}{\partial \ } = g\left(\frac{\pi_i(x,x)\pi_i(0,x)'(\ ) - \pi_i(0,x)(\ )\pi_i(x,x)'(\ )}{(\pi_i(x,x)(\ ) - \pi_i(0,x)(\ ))^2}\right)$ is negative if and only if $\frac{\pi_i(0,x)'}{\pi_i(0,x)} < \frac{\pi_i(x,x)'}{\pi_i(x,x)}$ since $(\pi_i(x,x)(\ ) - \pi_i(0,x)(\ ))^2 \neq 0$ for $\ < \bar{\ }$. This inequality holds for $\ < \bar{\ }$.

3. $\frac{\partial(1-b_{sym})\pi_i(x,x)}{\partial \ } = \frac{((\pi_i(x,x)(\ ) - \pi_i(0,x)(\ ))^2 + g\pi_i(0,x)(\ ))\pi_i(x,x)'(\ ) - g\pi_i(x,x)(\ )\pi_i(0,x)'(\ )}{(\pi_i(x,x)(\ ) - \pi_i(0,x)(\ ))^2}$ is negative if:

   $\frac{\pi_i(0,x)'}{\pi_i(0,x)} < \frac{\pi_i(x,x)'}{\pi_i(x,x)}$ (which is true from part 2) and if $g < \tilde{g}$ where

   $\tilde{g} \equiv \frac{(\pi_i(x,x)(\ ) - \pi_i(0,x)(\ ))^2 \pi_i(x,x)'(\ )}{\pi_i(x,x)(\ )\pi_i(0,x)'(\ ) - \pi_i(0,x)(\ )\pi_i(x,x)'(\ )}$, which is true since $\tilde{g} > \Delta \pi_{sym} > g$.

∎

Proof. Proposition 4: Define $RHS \equiv \frac{(\pi_i(x,x) + \pi_i(0,x))}{2\pi_i(x,x)}$ and $LHS \equiv \frac{\partial \pi_i(0,x)}{\partial \ } / \frac{\partial \pi_i(x,x)}{\partial \ }$

Since for $\ < \bar{\ }$, $\Delta \pi_{asym} > 0$ and $\Delta \pi_{sym} > 0$, there is a g low enough that the principal can induce innovation in stage 2.

Condition 8 holds if $g < g_{sym}$ where $g_{sym} = \frac{(\pi_i(x,x) - \pi_i(0,x))^2}{\pi_i(x,x)}$.

Condition 9 holds if $g < g_0$ where $g_0 = \frac{(\pi_i(x,0) - \pi_i(0,0))^2}{\pi_i(x,0)}$.

The negation of 10 holds if $g < g_{asym}$ where $g_{asym} = \frac{(\pi_j(x,0) - \pi_j(0,x))(\pi_i(x,x) - \pi_i(0,x))}{\pi_j(x,0)}$.

Since $g_{sym} < g_0$, $g_{sym} < g_{asym}$, and $g_{sym} < \Delta \pi_{sym}$, if $g < g_{sym}$ then the unique equilibrium is both owners inducing both managers to invest; furthermore, it is an equilibrium for both firms to invest only if $g < g_{sym}$.

$\frac{\partial g_{sym}}{\partial \ } = \frac{\pi_i(x,x) - \pi_i(0,x)}{\pi_i(x,x)^2}\left((\pi_i(x,x) + \pi_i(0,x))\frac{\partial \pi_i(x,x)}{\partial \ } - 2\pi_i(x,x)\frac{\partial \pi_i(0,x)}{\partial \ }\right)$ which is $\gtreqless 0$ if: $RHS \lesseqgtr LHS$.

RHS is always positive and always decreasing. LHS is always positive but is decreasing if and only if ($x < \frac{1}{2}$ and $c < 1 - x$ and $\ < \ _g(c,x)$ for some $0 < \ _g(c,x) < \bar{\ }$). As $\ \to 0^+$, $\frac{\partial g_{sym}}{\partial \ } < 0$ since: $\lim_{\ \to 0^+} RHS = RHS|_{\ =0} = \frac{1}{2}\left(1 + \frac{(1-c)^2}{(1-c+x)^2}\right)$ and $\lim_{\ \to 0^+} LHS = LHS|_{\ =0} = \frac{1-c}{1-c+x}$ so that $(RHS - LHS)_{\ =0} = \frac{x^2}{2(1-c+x)^2} > 0$. As $\ \to \bar{\ }^-$, $\frac{\partial g_{sym}}{\partial \ } < 0$ since: $\lim_{\ \to \bar{\ }} RHS = RHS|_{\ =\bar{\ }} = \frac{1}{2}$ and $\lim_{\ \to \bar{\ }} LHS = LHS|_{\ =\bar{\ }} = 0$. Therefore, $\frac{\partial g_{sym}}{\partial \ }$ will begin and end negative but may become positive if the LHS decreases fast enough.

Using Mathematica's Cylindrical Algebraic Decomposition Algorithm, we find that there is a $\bar{c}(x)$ and $\bar{x} < 1/2$ such that if and only if $c < \bar{c}(x)$ and $x < \bar{x}$, then there are $\ _L$ and $\ _U$ such for $\ _L < \ < \ _U$, $\frac{\partial g_{sym}}{\partial \ } > 0$; otherwise $\frac{\partial g_{sym}}{\partial \ } < 0$, where $\ _L$, $\ _U$, $\bar{c}$, and $\bar{x}$ are defined as the roots of polynomial equations. Taking the derivatives of $\ _L$

26

and $_U$ results in further implicitly defined functions, which are similarly signed by the Cylindrical Algebraic Decomposition Algorithm. ■

References

[1] Arrow, Kenneth, J. 1962. "Economic Welfare and the Allocation of Resources for Invention." In *The Rate and Direction of Inventive Activity: Economic and Social Factors* (ed. R. Nelson). (NBER) Princeton University Press.

[2] Bester, Helmut, and Emmanuel Petrakis. 1993. "The Incentives for Cost Reduction in a Differentiated Industry." *International Journal of Industrial Organization* 11(4): 519-534.

[3] Brealey, Richard A., and Stewart C. Myers. 1988. *Principles of Corporate Finance* (3rd edn.) New York: McGraw Hill Book Company.

[4] Gans, Joshua and Scott Stern. 2003. The Product Market and the Market for 'Ideas': Commercialization Strategies for Technology Entrepreneurs. *Research Policy.* 32(2): 333-350.

[5] Hall, Brian, and Jeffrey Liebman. 1998. "Are CEOs Really Paid Like Bureaucrats?" *Quarterly Journal of Economics*, 113(3): 653-691.

[6] Hall, Brian J., and Kevin J. Murphy. 2003. "The Trouble with Stock Options." *Journal of Economic Perspectives* 17(3): 49-70.

[7] Hart, Oliver. 1983. "The Market Mechanism as an Incentive Scheme." *Bell Journal of Economics*, 14(2): 366-82.

[8] Holderness, Clifford G., Randall S. Kroszner, and Dennis P. Sheehan. 1999. "Were the Good Old Days That Good? Changes in Managerial Stock Ownership since the Great Depression." *Journal of Finance* 54(2): 435-469.

[9] Holmstrom, Bengt, and Paul Milgrom. 1987. "Aggregation and linearity in the provision of intertemporal incentives." *Econometrica* 55: 303-28.

[10] Holmstrom, Bengt, and Paul Milgrom. 1991. "Multitask Principal-Agent Analyses: Incentive Contracts, Asset Ownership, and Job Design." *Journal of Law, Economics, and Organization* 7: 24-52.

[11] Piccolo, Salvatore, Marcello D'Amato, and Riccardo Martina. 2008. "Product Market Competition and Organizational Slack under Profit-Target Contracts." *International Journal of Industrial Organization* 26(6): 1389-1406.

[12] Prendergast, Canice. 1999. "The Provision of Incentives in Firms." *Journal of Economic Literature*, 37:7-63.

[13] Qiu, Larry. 1997. "On the Dynamic Efficiency of Bertrand and Cournot Equilibria." *Journal of Economic Theory*, 75: 213-229.

[14] Raith, Michael. 2003. "Competition, Risk, and Managerial Incentives." *American Economic Review*, 93(1):1425-1436.

[15] Scharftstein, David. 1988. "Product-market Competition and Managerial Slack." *RAND Journal of Economics*, 19(1): 147-155.

[16] Schmidt, Klaus. 1997. "Managerial Incentives and Product Market Competition." *Review of Economic Studies*, 64: 191-213.

[17] Schumpeter, Joseph. 1947. *Capitalism, Socialism and Democracy* (2nd edn.) London: Allen and Unwin.

[18] Tirole. Jean. 1988. *The Theory of Industrial Organization*. Cambridge, MA, The MIT Press.

[19] Vives, Xavier. 2008. "Innovation and Competitive Pressure." *Journal of Industrial Economics* 56(3): 419-469.

www.ingramcontent.com/pod-product-compliance
Lightning Source LLC
Chambersburg PA
CBHW081247170526
45165CB00009B/3226